*"The world has never been more competitive,
but it's no excuse for us to not teach love at a fundamental level."*

- Andy Croxson

Written by: Charles Dunrod
Illustrated by: Tatum Croft

First published in 2025 by Vektor Publishing
ISBN: 978-1-83709-075-4
Text copyright © Charles Dunrod, 2025
Illustration Copyright © Tatum Croft, 2025

All rights reserved. No part of this publication may be reproduced,
stored in a retrieval system, or transmitted in any form or by any means—
electronic, mechanical, photocopying, recording, or otherwise—without the prior written permission of the author,
except in the case of brief quotations used in reviews, educational settings, or scholarly work.

Printed in locations served by IngramSpark's global print network.
A copy of this publication is available from the British Library.
The moral rights of the author and illustrator have been asserted.
This is a work of fiction. Any resemblance to actual persons (living or deceased)
or real events is purely coincidental.

For more information, visit @boketto_immersed on Instagram

What Flutters Above

Charles Dunrod — Tatum Croft

She recently moved into a new house with her mum and dad.

She is eager to make some friends.

It is break time at her new school. All the children excitedly scurry from their classrooms and out into the bright sunny playground.

Athena feels a bit nervous, as she doesn't know anyone yet, she's unsure of who to play with. She sees a group of children playing and laughing together.

Athena decides to walk over to the cheerful children. One of the girls from the group of children notices her.

"Hi! Are you new?" asks the girl, eagerly.

"Yes, I just moved here." Athena says nervously.

"Wow, you're brand new then!" The girl says excitedly.

"My name is June!" she adds.

"My name is Athena" Athena responds.
"Would you like to play with us?" June asks. Athena nods happily.

"Let's play tag!" shouts Jin.
"I'm it!" shouts Zara. All of the kids scream and run away from Zara. Zara tags Connor.

Connor is very fast, right behind Athena.

Connor yells "Tag!"

In his excitement, he accidentally shoves Athena when tagging her. Athena then falls over grazing her knee.

"Your blood is red and underneath is pink?"
Connor says, looking very confused.

All the children look at Connor, looking just as confused.

The bell began to roar. Break time was over. As they are walking towards the main entrance, Athena and Ibrahim ask Connor what he meant before.

Connor puts his arm next to Athena's and points out the difference in their skin colour.

All the children are now in class. Athena feels upset and thinks she is worth **less** because of the colour of her skin.

She had never thought about skin colour mattering before today.

All the kids leave the school and wait patiently in the playground for their parents to arrive.

Connor's dad arrives. He sees his son with the remaining group of children and scowls. He notices Athena's graze on her knee.

"Everyone, this is my Dad." Says Connor. All the children smile and say hello.

"I don't want you playing with them." Connor's dad says.

All of the children froze, unsure of what Connor's dad meant by that.

"But... but, they're my friends! They've been really nice to me today." Connor says, sadly.

"They may have been nice today, but they are..."

"TROUBLE!" He says, coldly.

"She's obviously trouble, look at her." Connor's dad says pointing to Athena's injured knee.

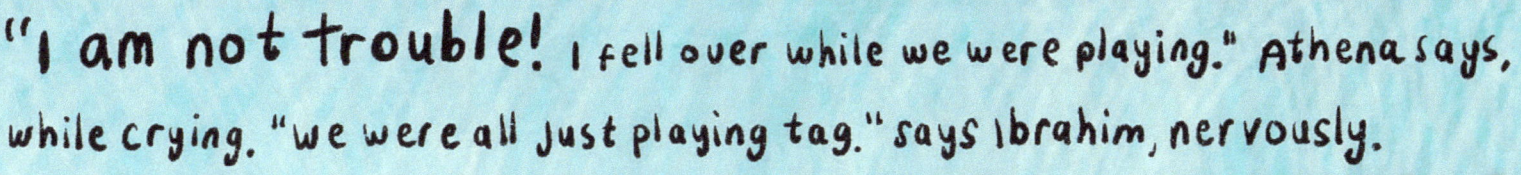

"I am not trouble! I fell over while we were playing." Athena says, while crying. "We were all just playing tag." says Ibrahim, nervously.

"What you were doing doesn't matter. None of you should be here anyway." He says, harshly.

"I don't want you talking to their sort." He shouts sharply, pulling him away.

"Maybe it has something to do with what he said about Athena earlier. Connor pointed out how they have **different skin colours**." Mateo says.

"Skin colour? Why does skin colour matter?" Ibrahim asks.
"It doesn't, does it?" Athena asks, while wiping away a tear.

All the children shrug in confusion. June hugs Athena and the other children tell her not to worry. All the children's parents arrived, they said goodbye and went home.

Athena shuffled into her house, feeling very confused and upset. Her mum walks in from the kitchen and kisses her on the forehead. "How was your day, sweetheart?" asks Athena's mum.

Athena looks back at her mum, with a small tear falling down her cheek.

"It wasn't how I thought it would be." She said gently.

Athena's dad strolled in overhearing what Athena had said.

"Oh? Is it something to do with your knee?" Her dad asks as he takes his coat off, puts Athena's bag down, and sits on the sofa with her and her mum.

Her dad's expression changed. His face was no longer blank, a smile slipped through.

"The colour of your skin does not matter, **who you are** and **what you do** is the most important thing."

"Treat others how you want to be treated." Said her dad.

"But the things Connor and his dad said... It made me feel like I'm not worth as much because of my skin colour." She said sadly.

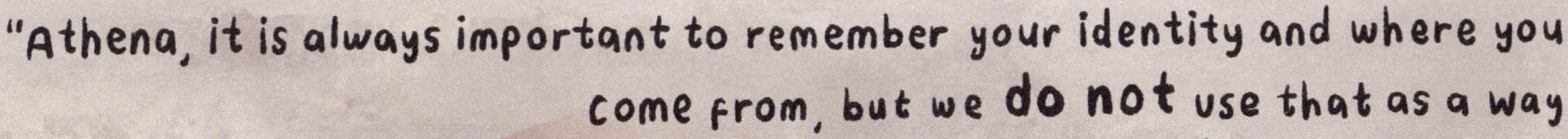

"Athena, it is always important to remember your identity and where you come from, but we do not use that as a way to judge a person."

"I'm black and my roots come from the Caribbean. I am proud of my background."

"Who you are is who you choose to be. You are no less of a human because of your skin colour, you are unique and beautiful." He smiled.

"Don't worry about these people, honey. They have a lot of learning to do.

Try not to think bad of Connor, it isn't his fault. What he has said is learnt behaviour from his dad." Says her mum.

Athena's dad grins. "We need to get you to bed" he says.

Athena hugs her parents and wanders upstairs to get ready for bed.

Athena begins to drift off into a deep sleep,

...to the land of dreams she goes.

The air is **thick** and the sky is dark. Athena feels strange.

Fog crept its way in.

Athena froze, as the air became **cold**.

Out of the mist appears a **figure**.

It was Connor's dad.

Athena could feel her heart **beating** hard like a drum, trying to escape her chest.

"Oh look, A TROUBLE MAKER."
Says Connor's dad. Athena becomes scared, and tries to run, but wherever she turned ...he was there.

"Trouble!"
"Go away!"
Echoes each clone of Connor's dad.

"PLEASE STOP!" Shouts Athena, with tears trailing down her face.

The comments cornered Athena, it became darker and darker.

"Athena, wake up!" said a soft voice.

Athena opened her eyes and she was in her bed.

It was all a dream... Athena thought.

She looked around the room and saw her mum, opening the window.

A small butterfly flutters into Athena's room. It's colour was black. It fluttered over Athena and then flew back out of the window.

"Mum, I keep seeing butterflies whenever something bad happens and they are losing their colour each time. What does it mean?" Athena asks, as she sits up in her bed.

"They say if a butterfly flaps its wings at a certain time, in a certain place, it will cause a hurricane somewhere in the world.

Everything affects everything, sweetie." Athena's mum said softly.

It is almost the end of school.
Athena and her friends are in their final lesson.
The teacher has them all sat in a large circle.

"Okay class, I thought it would be a good idea for everyone to learn a valuable skill. I have asked for our local paramedics to join us today to teach you something important!" Says Mr Hall.

Two paramedics walk into the class. One is black and the other is from East Asia.

"Hi guys, my name is Muna and this is my colleague, Mei." Says the black paramedic. All the children wave.

The paramedics opened a large bag they brought with them. "Today we are going to teach you a little first aid, mainly how to safely help someone who is choking." says Mei as she places a dummy on the table and inserts a small object into its mouth.

"When someone is choking, they are unable to speak or breathe. It is important that you go behind them." Says Muna.
Mei is behind the dummy and demonstrates 5 back blows between the shoulder blades.
Mei then demonstrates 5 abdominal thrusts.

"Now, this last bit is **important**. You then need to pull your hands **inwards** and **up** at the same time. Be careful not to squeeze the ribs, it is very harmful. Mei will show you how." Muna says with a big smile.

All the children are focused on Mei's hands. The object shoots out of the dummy's mouth.

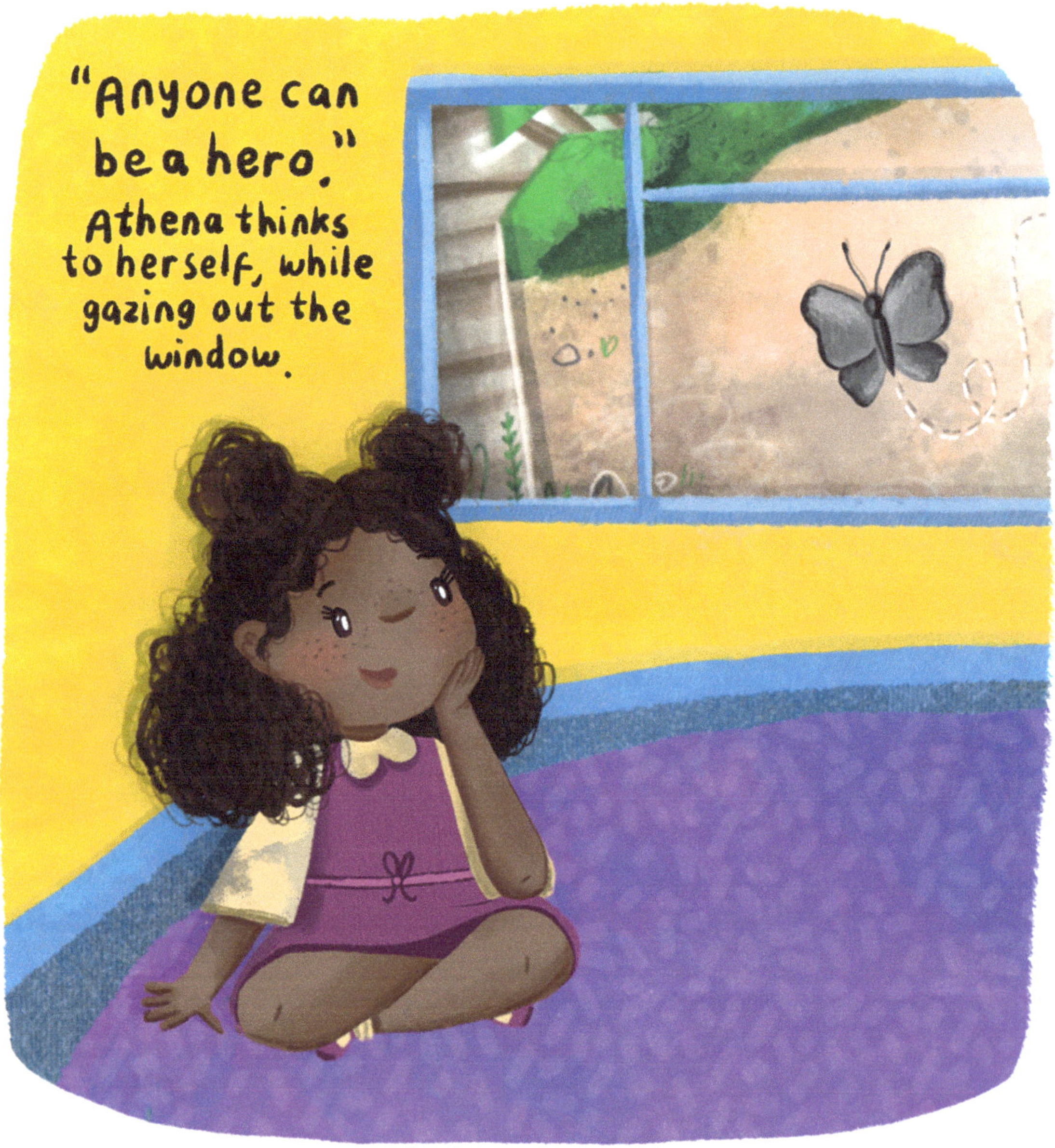
"Anyone can be a hero."
Athena thinks to herself, while gazing out the window.

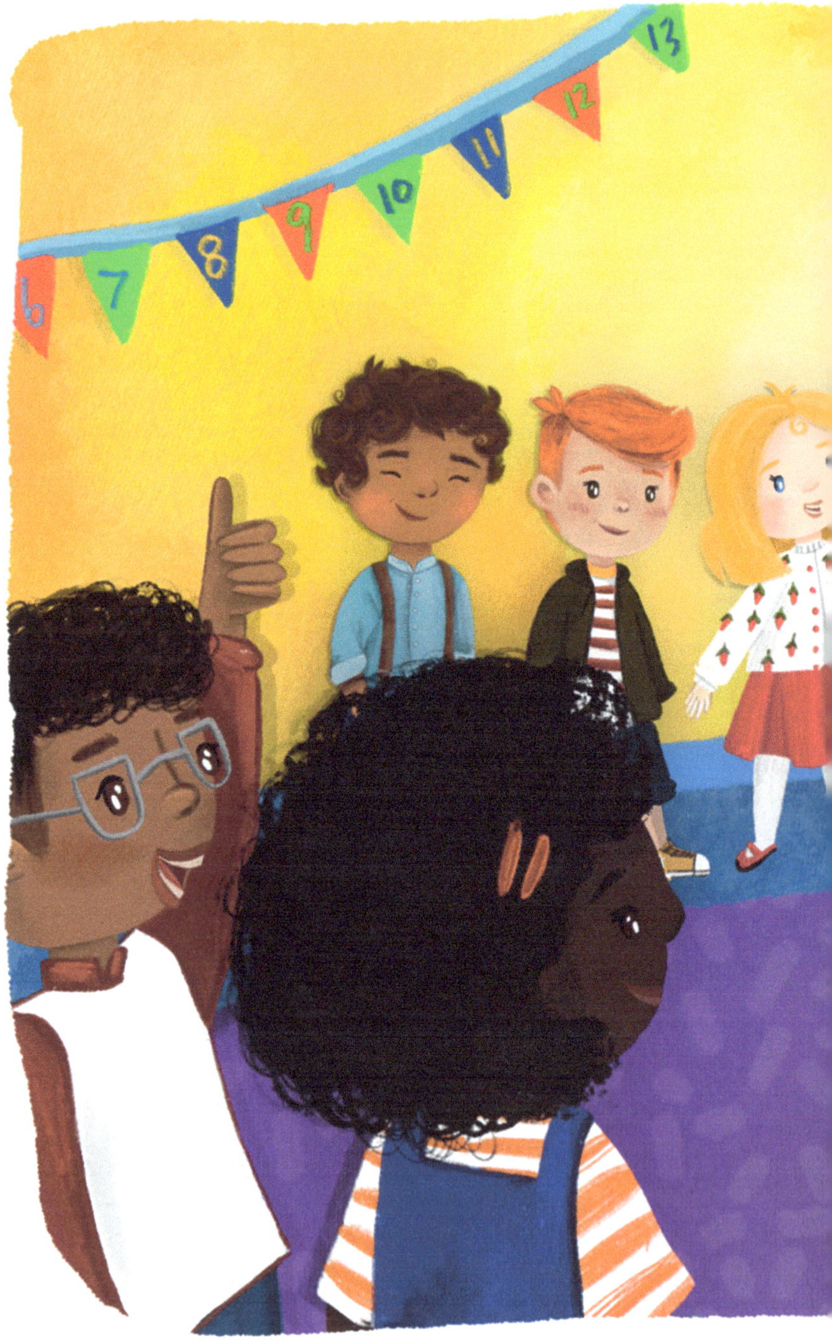
6 7 8 9 10 11 12 13

The event inspired Athena and showed her that skin colour **does not** stop anyone from doing great things.

The children get into small groups and practice the move with the paramedics. Athena has a try. She does 5 back blows between the shoulders, then 5 abdominal thrusts and the object flies out of the dummies mouth.

"Well done Athena!" yells Zara and Jin.

Athena's smile grows even wider and brighter. "Thank you, guys!" She howls with excitement.

Athena's dad arrives at the school gates. He walks over to Athena and June. They both smile at Athena's dad. "Oh no, it's Connor and his dad." June says, suddenly.

Athena is silent. Her dad rubs her on the head, smiles and walks over to Connor's dad. He mentions the comments he and his son had made to Athena and her friends.

"There is nothing wrong with what me or my son said. You all don't have any right being here." His dad says, with a dull expression.

Connor looks shocked at his dad, while holding onto an apple.

Athena's dad is horrified. "How can you say that, we are all equal." He says. "Dad, please stop!" Connor says, fearfully.

"That's not true. My boy was picked on in his last school because he's ginger!" Connor's dad says angrily, ignoring Connor. Athena's dad looks cross. "But you're doing the same thing to all of us." June says anxiously.

Connor takes a big bite out of his apple, while trying to pull his dad away.

"Your sort has never done any good and never will." Connor's dad says, coldly.

Athena's dad and all the children are shocked over the comment. Connor's dad starts to walk away and tells Connor that they are leaving.

Suddenly, Connor does not look too good...

He begins to cough and choke.

"Connor! Someone help." Connor's dad yells in panic.

Everyone remains still...

"We never do anything good, right?" Says Zara.

Connor's face turns blue.

Athena freezes.

She remembers what she had learned. She then rushes behind, wraps her arms around him and performs first aid.

Athena gives Connor 5 back blows between the shoulder blades like she was taught.

She pulls Connor's stomach in and upon the third pull Connor spits out the apple chunk that was stuck in his throat, and gasps for air.

As Athena lets go of Connor, he instantly turns around to hug her.

"You saved me! Thank you!" Connor says, overjoyed.

Everyone smiles.
Athena's dad shakes his hand.

"No need to feel down.
You see what you couldn't see before."
Athena's dad says with a smile.

All the families cook and bring traditional dishes from their homes to the park, as well as music and other items from their cultures

to give connor's dad a **larger view** of what other cultures have to offer.

Note from the Author

I wrote *What Flutters Above* as the book I needed when I was growing up.
As a child, I experienced racism, discrimination and experiences that made me question my worth and place in the world. This story is my way of telling every child who feels different: You are and will always be enough.

For more information visit
@boketto_immersed on instagram

Parents and caregivers need to understand that the early years of childhood development are the most crucial point in a person's life. These years significantly influence how a child perceives themselves and the world. That's why it's so important to nurture these stages with care, understanding, and unconditional love at every opportunity.

To the readers, this book is for you.
Being different does not make you less important than others. Be gentle and kind with those around you, but also be proud of who you are. Stand up for yourself and take responsibility for your actions. You are enough. Always.
My core as a human is kindness.

To A & J, no matter the distance between us, whether physical, emotional, or shaped by the mindsets of others, you will always be my most precious adventure. I will love you, always.

Note from the Illustrator

I have always been drawn to the importance of using beautiful imagery to shine a light on topics dear to my heart. Whether it be raising awareness about diversity, education, health or self-acceptance, I believe children's books have a responsibility to introduce these topics to little ones in a way that is fun, playful, and digestible.

It is an honour working with authors who have such important messages to share with the world, and even more of an honour I am able to help bring them to life with my illustrations.

As a mum of two little ones, I am proud to help spread positivity and love through the books I have illustrated and I am so happy to be a part of an ever growing library of diversity and inclusivity in children's picture books.

To my beautiful family - Thank you for always supporting me and showing me that love, creativity, and growth have no bounds. You inspire the work I do, always.

Tatum Croft

Website: www.tatumcroft.co.uk
Instagram: @tatumcroftillustration
Etsy shop: TatumCroftUK

For business enquiries email me at tatumcroft@yahoo.co.uk

www.ingramcontent.com/pod-product-compliance
Lightning Source LLC
Chambersburg PA
CBHW042001070526

44584CB00005BA/315